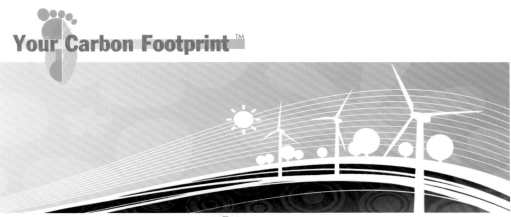

Your Carbon Footprint™

On the Move
Green Transportation

Kathy Furgang and Adam Furgang

rosen publishing's
rosen
central®

New York

To Ben and Caleb

Published in 2009 by The Rosen Publishing Group, Inc.
29 East 21st Street, New York, NY 10010

Library of Congress Cataloging-in-Publication Data

Furgang, Kathy.
On the move: green transportation / Kathy Furgang and Adam Furgang.
    p. cm.—(Your carbon footprint)
Includes bibliographical references and index.
ISBN-13: 978-1-4042-1773-7 (library binding)
1. Transportation—Environmental aspects—Juvenile literature. I. Furgang, Adam.
II. Title.
HE147.65.F87 2009
388'.049—dc22

                                                                    2008000677

Manufactured in the United States of America

On the cover: Top left: A middle school student in Tully, New York, locks up his bicycle after riding to school. Top right: A man fills up his car at a biodiesel station in Berkeley, California. Bottom: A solar-powered vehicle races along the highway in Kingman, Arizona.

Contents

Introduction

Think for a moment about all of the things that make life easier and more comfortable today compared to hundreds of years ago. We have cars, trucks, computers, factories, airplanes, and ships. We have heating and air conditioning for our homes. We even have heating and air conditioning for our cars. What makes all of these things possible? The answer is fossil fuels.

For many years now, fossil fuels have allowed us to make the energy we need to run factories, make electricity, and heat and cool our homes. Fossil fuels such as oil, coal, and natural gas are formed under Earth's surface. They come from the ancient remains of plants and animals. When fossil fuels are removed from the earth and burned, they produce energy. Since the Industrial Revolution of the 1800s, we humans have come to rely more and more on fossil fuels for our energy.

Fossil fuels are far from an ideal energy source, however. When they are burned for energy, they produce a gas called carbon dioxide, which is sent into the atmosphere. With increased carbon dioxide in the air, more of the sun's heat gets trapped in Earth's atmosphere, causing it to warm up. This gradual warming of Earth's atmosphere is called global warming. Many scientists believe that we have burned so much fossil fuel that global warming is causing a change in Earth's climate.

It's natural for Earth's climate to change. But scientists say it has been warming much more rapidly than what is natural. In the past 100 years, the average temperature of the planet has increased by about 1 degree Fahrenheit (0.6 degrees Celsius). This may not sound like a lot, but it is a large increase for such a short period of time in Earth's 4.5-billion-year history.

Just by living in our modern society, we all contribute to the high levels of carbon dioxide in the air. The term "carbon footprint" has come to refer to the amount of carbon dioxide a person, group, corporation,

The amount of gasoline a personal vehicle consumes is just one factor used to calculate one's overall carbon footprint.

or even a nation sends into the air. Carbon footprints are measured in pounds of carbon dioxide gas. For example, Kim may produce about 40,000 pounds (18,144 kilograms) of carbon dioxide per year. This figure is typical for most Americans. How does Kim heat her home? How many plane trips has she gone on in the past year? How many times has she filled her car's gas tank? How often does she run her air conditioner during the summer? Answers to these questions would be used to calculate Kim's carbon footprint. You can visit the Web site of the Environmental Protection Agency (www.epa.gov/climatechange/emissions/ind_calculator.html) to calculate your own carbon footprint.

An exact carbon footprint is impossible to measure. The term is mainly used as a way to point people, businesses, and large corporations toward "greener" (more environmentally sound) practices. The hope is that knowing about a carbon footprint will make people more aware of things they can do to reduce it. For example, we can now get energy from wind, water, and the sun. Unlike fossil fuels, these renewable energy sources do not produce carbon dioxide as a waste. So, making use of them will reduce your carbon footprint. Read on to find out about some simple things you can do to reduce the size of your carbon footprint when it comes to getting from place to place.

How You
Can Help

How much carbon dioxide is produced by your daily activities? That is the basic idea behind a carbon footprint. If your activities use a lot of fossil fuel, you probably have a large carbon footprint. You cannot see your carbon footprint, but it's there, like an imaginary shadow. A person or object with no carbon footprint at all is called carbon neutral. In our modern society, it is almost impossible to be carbon neutral, but you can strive to have as small a carbon footprint as possible. Ultimately, this will help curb the effects of global warming.

Why Is Global Warming a Problem?

You may be asking, "What effect does global warming have on me?" After all, small average global temperature increases will hardly be noticed. In fact, global warming is already having an impact on our planet. For example, increased global temperatures affect the weather. According to the U.S. Environmental Protection Agency, more natural disasters, droughts, floods, and extreme storms such as hurricanes and tsunamis occurred in the past fifty years than at any other time in recorded history. Increasing temperatures are also

Wildfires are more intense in areas affected by droughts. Fires often threaten nearby communities, causing people to evacuate their homes.

causing intense dry spells and droughts across the globe, affecting all local plant and animal life—including humans.

Along coastlines, global warming may have an opposite effect. Glaciers in the Arctic are melting faster than ever before. These melting ice caps cause sea levels to rise. In turn, coastal cities around the world, including New York, Seattle, Miami, and Hong Kong, may become flooded. Life in inland areas will be affected, too. For example,

The Power of a Bicycle

Riding bicycles is often thought of as something kids do for fun. But a bicycle offers a great way for a person of any age to stay in shape while helping the environment. Portland, Oregon, is considered one of the most environmentally friendly biking cities in the United States. Portland has 164 miles (264 kilometers) of bicycle lanes, 66 miles (106 km) of bicycle paths, and 30 miles (48 km) of bicycle roads with low car volume. With public facilities like these, reducing one's carbon footprint can be easy, fun, and good for your health. Ask in your town about bicycle paths and how they can be used.

Bike lanes in Portland, Oregon, provide people with an alternative to using fossil fuels to get around town.

scientists predict the glaciers in Montana's Glacier National Park will melt within the next twenty years. When the glaciers are gone, thousands of people will have lost an important freshwater supply.

You May Already Be Helping

The way we get from place to place is an important part of figuring out our carbon footprint. Reducing the amount of fossil fuel we use while traveling can be a challenge, but young people often help without even realizing it. Since younger teens cannot drive cars, they often walk or use skateboards, bicycles, inline skates, or foot scooters to get around. These methods of travel do not require fossil fuel, so they are a great carbon-neutral way to get from one place to another.

Once you understand the concept of a carbon footprint, it's important to spread the word. If your friends are not yet trying to reduce their own carbon footprints, explain to them why it is important. Think about the difference ten people can make compared to just one person!

Sometimes, you will have to go farther than your skateboard will take you. For example, getting to and from school might require you to ride in vehicles powered by gasoline, a refined fossil fuel. In this case, riding a school bus is a good way for young people to limit carbon emissions. Imagine if every student on the bus was driven to school separately. Each student would represent a car engine that had to be started and distance that had to be traveled. Having a bus pick up many students along a route is much more economical and saves on gasoline.

School buses are a better option than individual cars, but they still produce carbon emissions and add to your carbon footprint. If you really want to minimize school bus carbon dioxide emissions, check into the company that operates school buses in your district. Working with a teacher, school administrator, environmental club, or a parents' council representative, contact the bus company and ask the bus company to consider ways to reduce harmful bus emissions, if it isn't doing so already.

Replacing older buses with newer ones that meet stricter emissions standards is an expensive solution. However, there are some less expensive measures that can be taken. For example, the carbon footprint

Every day, approximately 24 million students in the United States take the bus to and from school.

of the bus will be smaller if the bus is well maintained. A smoother running bus with properly inflated tires saves on gasoline because the vehicle operates more efficiently. Also, bus mechanics could put devices on the engines and exhaust systems to reduce exhaust pollution. Finally, idling, or keeping the bus running while waiting for students to load, is a total waste of gasoline. Ask the bus company to make sure its drivers do not idle unnecessarily.

City Kids

Where you live may affect how you think about your carbon footprint. For example, kids who live in big cities will have easier access to public transportation than kids who live in rural areas and thus have to take individual cars to get places. Large cities usually offer a variety of inexpensive ways to get around. If you happen to live in a city or urban area where such transportation is available, just making use of it is a great way to reduce your carbon footprint.

Think Before You Act

For short trips around your neighborhood, walking or riding a bike is the best way to travel. However, you should always keep safety a top priority. There will be times when walking or riding is not the wisest choice. For instance, if it is raining or snowing, or if it is too hot or too cold, it's probably wiser to take a car or a bus.

Having a lot to carry, such as sports equipment, is another factor that could interfere with walking or self-powered travel. Biking to a football game with heavy equipment is not practical and it could be dangerous. Similarly, trying to walk to school in the morning with many books or a large band instrument could also cause problems.

Do not avoid certain modes of travel only because they add to your carbon footprint. Think about what makes sense. Reducing your carbon footprint should not put you in danger or cause you to take all day to get from one place to another.

A carpool works like a small-scale school bus. The riders come from different homes, but they are all headed to the same destination.

Think About a Carpool

If you must be driven to school each day, think about organizing a carpool. That way, several people will be picked up in one car, similar to the way a bus works. Here are a few ideas about carpooling:

- Ask students at school how they get there each day. If some friends who live nearby are driven to school by a parent, try to organize a carpool.

- Once your carpool is up and running, make sure the parents take the shortest route to school. You can help by looking up routes online or using a map of your area.
- Encourage the parent who is driving to take care of a few chores along the way. This will keep fuel from being wasted later while taking the same route. Leaving home a few minutes early may be all that is needed to accomplish this.
- Make sure the tires on the family car are inflated properly. Your parents can help with this the next time the car goes for scheduled maintenance. Slightly deflated tires contribute to a car having higher fuel consumption.

If a carpool is just not possible, do not worry—there are plenty of other ways you can cut down on your carbon emissions.

2 Greener Car Travel

I n the early 1900s, Henry Ford's Model T became the first affordable car for most Americans. Demand was so high for these cars that Ford began to produce them on assembly lines in 1914. In a matter of just a few years, millions of Ford Model Ts were on the road. This was the start of the automobile age in America.

Today, the United States is the largest market in the world for cars and passenger vehicles. In 2005, there were more than 247 million vehicles registered in the United States alone. There are nearly 4 million miles (6.4 million kilometers) of roadway throughout the country. With figures like these, it is no wonder that use of fossil fuels has become a problem. When we think about reducing our transportation carbon footprint, car use is a great place to start.

Helpful Car Tips

Cars are such an important part of our American lifestyle that getting rid of them entirely to cut down on carbon dioxide emissions is next to impossible. So, the next best thing is to think about how to use our cars in smarter ways.

If you drive, reducing the size of your car goes a long way toward reducing your carbon footprint. This Smart Car is extremely fuel-efficient—and easy to park.

Leave the Car at Home

When it makes sense to do so, encourage your family to leave the car at home. Walking or bike riding is good exercise and will provide an opportunity for you to slow down and see your neighborhood and meet neighbors. It will also save money on gasoline and may even allow the family car to last longer.

Keep It Small

Large cars, SUVs, minivans, and small trucks are popular family vehicles because they can carry many people and a lot of cargo. With their increased size and weight, however, larger vehicles burn more gasoline than smaller cars traveling the same distance.

If your family has both a larger car and a smaller one, think about how each one is used. You should use the smaller car when just one or two family members are going somewhere. Use the larger car only when necessary—for instance, when a lot of people are traveling together or when you are carrying luggage, bicycles, or other large or heavy cargo. Sometimes, it is necessary and practical to drive a larger car, and other times it is wasteful to do so.

Think Ahead

Use less gasoline by making only one trip in the car to do your family errands. If you or your parents have to pick up things at three stores during the week, for example, plan the shortest route past each of the stores and get the job done all in one trip.

Carpools and High-Occupancy Vehicles

Carpooling cuts down on the number of cars on the road. Many large cities and major highways encourage people to organize carpools. During the morning and afternoon rush hours, carpool lanes—also called high-occupancy vehicle lanes—go into effect. At these times, cars carrying only the driver are not allowed to travel in the special lanes. So, in addition to reducing their carbon footprints, carpoolers

Check on busy highways for carpool signs. The diamond symbol on the sign is also painted on the pavement to indicate which lane is designated for carpoolers.

face less traffic and get to where they are going faster.

Don't Let the Car Run

If you are waiting in the car to pick up a friend or your brother or sister, remind the driver to turn off the engine if you will be waiting awhile. An idling car burns fuel, emitting carbon dioxide. Shutting the car off while you wait will cut down on unnecessary carbon dioxide emissions. But do this only if you will be waiting for more than a couple of minutes. The gasoline it takes to restart the car may be greater than the amount it would use while idling for just a couple of minutes.

Fuel Economy

In the United States, "gas mileage" describes how many miles a car can travel on one gallon of gas. A car that gets good gas mileage saves money. It also runs efficiently and gives off less carbon dioxide than a car that does not get good gas mileage.

It's easy to figure out the gas mileage of your family car. Next time your car's gas tank is full, ask if you can reset the car's trip odometer (a special mile counter on the dashboard). Then, when the tank is empty

Measuring Fuel Efficiency

The concept of "gas mileage" isn't very useful if you measure distances in kilometers rather than miles. Sometimes, people refer to the kilometrage of a car. More common, however, is to calculate the number of liters of fuel needed to travel 100 kilometers (L/100km). Using this system, a car that gets 30 miles to the gallon needs about 7.8 liters to travel 100 kilometers (7.8 L/100 km). A lower number would indicate even better fuel efficiency.

and needs to be filled again, check the trip odometer. This tells you how many miles your car traveled on one tank of gas. Also note how many gallons were pumped to fill the tank. You now have all the information that you need. Divide the number of miles traveled by the number of gallons pumped to find out your car's approximate gas mileage. For example, if the car drove 250 miles (402 km) and used 10 gallons (38 L) of gas, the car is getting 25 miles (40 km) to the gallon. (The formula: $250 \div 10 = 25$.) This number will change from fill-up to fill-up, depending on the type of driving that was done. Highway driving results in better gas mileage than city driving.

When you find out what your approximate gas mileage is, talk with your parents about how you can improve it on the next tank of gas. Here are some ideas that you can suggest:

- Take good care of your vehicle. A tuned-up motor uses less gas.
- Replace dirty air and fuel filters.

- Avoid running the air conditioner. (Car heaters, on the other hand, usually do not affect gas mileage too much.)
- Use a tire gauge regularly to make sure your tires are properly inflated. Most tires should be inflated to 30 to 35 pounds per square inch (207–241 kilopascals).
- Drive on highways rather than city streets whenever possible. Vehicles running at constant speeds burn gas more efficiently than those that stop and go often.
- Remove unnecessary cargo. Extra weight in the car lowers gas mileage.
- Drive the speed limit on the highway. Most cars operate very efficiently at 55 to 65 miles per hour (89–105 km per hour) but lose gas mileage at higher or lower speeds.

Hybrid Cars

Any vehicle that relies on two or more power sources is a hybrid vehicle. Most of today's hybrid cars use a traditional gasoline engine along with an electric motor powered by batteries. Hybrid vehicles are designed to save fuel. Because of this, you will see hybrid cars with sleeker designs than some other cars. A teardrop shape, for example, reduces the dragging force of wind on the car, conserving gasoline.

Hybrid cars may not be the right choice for every family or situation. Hybrids tend to have less cargo space because room is taken up by the batteries that store the electric energy that is generated while driving. Hybrids can also be more expensive compared to some smaller, fuel-efficient cars that use only gas.

Hybrid SUVs are a reality. In the 2006 Ford Mercury Mariner Hybrid, the large rechargeable battery is stored under the spacious cargo area.

New models of hybrid cars are becoming available all the time. If more people choose hybrid cars as their vehicles, they will send a very powerful message to the car companies to produce more eco-friendly cars. In 2006, U.S. consumers bought more than 250,000 hybrid cars. That was up about 50,000 from the year before, but these numbers could still be improved. Only about 1.5 percent of the cars on the road in the United States are hybrids.

Did You Know?

California leads the country in the number of hybrid cars sold. In 2006, more than 67,500 hybrid vehicles were sold in the state. Nearly 31,000 of those hybrids were sold in the city of Los Angeles alone. This is good news for people living in Los Angeles, as the city has the worst air pollution in the country, according to the American Lung Association.

Hybrids are the most popular choice for people looking for an alternative to gasoline-only cars. But there are many other technologies that are being developed for consumer use, including biofuel, solar power, and hydrogen fuel cells. It's entirely possible that one day soon, a practical and affordable car will be available that does not rely on fossil fuel.

3 Public Transportation

Cars may be everywhere you look, but they aren't the only form of transportation that you can use. Public transportation is a kind of travel that is designed to move many people at one time. Buses, trains, subways, and even trolleys and trams are all examples of public transportation. Each of these methods contributes to our carbon footprint in some way.

No matter where you live, it helps to be familiar with the kinds of public transportation that are available to you. Your family may be on vacation in a city and be thinking about whether or not to take a bus or a subway. Or, your own town may have public transportation services that you are not even aware of. In this chapter, we will learn how public transportation can be used to reduce a carbon footprint.

Bus

Buses are the most common form of public transportation in the United States. Just about every developed area in the country has some sort of bus service. Local bus service can take you from one end of town to another, usually with scheduled stops along the route at shopping areas, museums, libraries, and

Many cities are replacing their older public buses with hybrid electric versions. They use less gasoline and emit less carbon dioxide than traditional buses.

other places. Long-distance bus trips take you out of town or to other faraway locations.

A trip on a bus will be more eco-friendly than one made in a personal car, simply because a bus carries a lot of people at once. In addition, some public bus companies are replacing their traditional buses with hybrids. New York City, for example, will have the world's largest fleet of diesel-electric hybrid buses by the year 2010. These buses run cleaner than older buses and emit less carbon dioxide.

Choosing the Best Way to Travel

If your family is planning a vacation, think about the best kind of public transportation for your trip. How far are you going? Does it make more sense to fly or take the train? Should you take a car or bus? Think about the amount of luggage you will be carrying and how you will get around once you reach your destination. These factors should all help you decide on the best way to keep your carbon footprint as small as possible.

Public buses are usually a very affordable mode of transportation, and most cities offer reduced bus fares to students. Before you ride, though, check with a bus company in your area to find out more about student fares and the rules of the local bus service. Also make sure you and your friends get your parents' permission to ride the bus.

Train

One of the most reliable ways to travel long distances over land is by train. Since the 1800s, trains have been used in the United States to carry cargo, goods, and people across the country. The earliest trains were powered by coal, which was burned to make a steam engine work. Today, most trains are either powered by diesel engines or electricity. Diesel engines release carbon dioxide, and it takes a lot of fossil fuel to produce electricity, so taking a train contributes to your carbon footprint. Even so, if you travel by train instead of by car, you greatly reduce your output of carbon. Let's say you have a 7-mile (11 km) daily commute. If you leave the car at home and take a high-occupancy diesel train instead, you reduce your annual carbon output by about 1,340 pounds (608 kg)!

Many suburban towns have reliable commuter train service that carries people back and forth to their jobs every day. You, too, can take these commuter trains between towns along the route. Check the schedules at local train stations to see where they go and when they arrive and depart. Local trains usually drop passengers off at popular stops, in the middle of town or near shops and restaurants. A train ride can be fun, too. Traveling by train gives you time to relax and do other things, such as reading or doing your homework. In addition, many trains have restrooms and dining cars for your convenience.

Subways

If you live in a larger city, you may be able to get around using an affordable "metro" rail system. New York and Boston, for example, have electric public rail systems. Using an electric metro rail system instead of a car for a 7-mile (11 km) commute reduces one's annual carbon emissions by a whopping 1,518 pounds (689 kg).

Sometimes, metro trains travel aboveground. But near the city center, they usually travel underground. In this way, subways help to relieve congestion and reduce exhaust pollution on city streets. The New York City metro transit system carries an average of 4.9 million riders throughout the city every weekday. In 2006, riders there took a total of 1.5 billion trips on the subway. Without the subway system, New York City would have many more cars on the road and far more pollution in the air.

Plane

Today, airplanes are a convenient way to travel long distances. Incredibly, a person can fly all the way around the world in only one and a half days! Planes are the fastest way to move a lot of people

Jet fuel exhaust pollutes the air near the earth's surface as well as the atmosphere miles above the earth.

a long distance in a short amount of time. However, planes can have quite a large carbon footprint. A Boeing 747 airplane, for example, burns about a gallon (3.8 L) of fuel every second. This translates to about 18,000 gallons (68,137 L) for a five-hour flight. That's about the amount of water that it would take to fill a good-sized swimming pool. A 747 can carry more than 500 people, which helps to reduce the amount of fuel used per person, but the plane still has a very large carbon footprint. Whenever possible, seek an alternative to airline travel.

Like cars, planes have become a necessary part of our modern society. Instead of cutting them out altogether, we can become aware of

Carbon Offset

"Carbon offset" is a term used to describe the actions you can take to balance out activities that produce carbon emissions. In effect, it means doing something good for the environment to make up for something that might be harmful to it. Carbon offset might be as simple as planting a tree every time you fly on a plane.

how to conserve fuel whenever possible. When private jets travel with only a few passengers at a time, the amount of fuel used per passenger is very great. To cut down on the effects that air travel has on the environment, planes should travel with as many passengers as possible. Waiting on standby at an airport to help fill up a plane is one way to reduce your overall carbon footprint.

Leonardo DiCaprio is a Hollywood star who is working to make people aware of wasteful habits that harm the environment. Although DiCaprio is a celebrity who can afford to fly in private jets, he says that he now travels on commercial planes whenever possible. This cuts out thousands of gallons of fuel that he may have consumed to take his own flight.

Large organizations, including NASA and Boeing, are working on hybrid airplane technologies that will consume less fossil fuel. Soon, we may be able to fly on hybrid planes, just as we can ride in hybrid cars.

Ridership on streetcars in Portland, Oregon, has more than doubled since 2001. The convenient electric trolleys make more than forty stops on their loop through the city.

Trolleys and Trams

Trolleys and trams are rail vehicles used for traveling short distances, usually within cities. Trolleys were popular in the early 1900s, but cars, subways, and buses eventually replaced them. Old-time trolleys moved using cables that were sometimes pulled by horses. Today, electric trolleys are making a comeback in cities, especially in Europe. London,

England; Frankfurt, Germany; and Warsaw, Poland, are cities that use electric trams.

As is the case with subways, the electricity used to power trams and trolleys is usually produced by a coal-burning power plant. So, even though electric-powered trams emit no carbon dioxide, this mode of transportation does contribute to your carbon footprint. But when it comes to reducing your carbon footprint, going by tram or trolley is a better alternative than traveling by personal car.

4 The Future of Transportation

Most forms of transportation today are still powered by carbon-based fuels. In order to reduce our carbon footprints and cut down on the effects of global warming, the transportation industry needs to find reliable and affordable alternatives to these carbon-based fuels. Progress is being made quickly, now that there is great demand for cleaner-running cars, buses, and planes.

Hybrid cars are available today, and other technologies are also being developed. Future car buyers (including you, probably) may have many alternatives to carbon-based fuels. It makes sense to know about these alternatives now.

If someone in your family is considering a new car or truck, talk to him or her about new technologies that are being developed for commercial vehicles. Or, visit a car dealer to discuss when a new kind of car will be available to the public. Dealers may be able to tell you what kind of gas mileage the car will have, how many people it will seat, and how much it might cost. These are all factors a family must consider when buying a car. Young, single drivers may have even more options, as they can usually buy smaller, more economical vehicles with less passenger and cargo room.

The top of this car is made of solar cells. The cells convert the energy from sunlight into electrical energy to power the car's motor.

Solar Power

Solar cars are not some science-fiction dream of the future. They exist today. However, none are practical enough for people to use for their everyday transportation needs. Solar energy requires panels, called cells, which absorb the sun's energy and convert it into electrical energy. Solar cells that are small enough to fit on a car cannot generate a lot of electricity. As a result, solar cars are typically light and small, usually with room enough for only one person.

Despite the limitations of solar cars, many solar vehicle competitions are held each year. Some attract teams from major car companies such as General Motors and Ford. Other competitions, like the Dell-Winston School Solar Car Challenge, are specifically for high school students. Sponsored by the Dell Computer Company, this contest teaches high school students about the technologies behind solar power. If you are interested in learning more about the Dell-Winston School Solar Car Challenge, go to the official Web site at www.winstonsolar.org.

Electricity

Electric cars that run off batteries have been around since before gasoline-powered cars. Unfortunately, battery technology was not good enough to make these cars practical for everyday use—until recently. Today, electric car technology is greatly improved. Some small electric vehicles, such as golf carts, forklifts, and even bicycles and scooters, make good use of current technologies. However, they do not travel long distances and usually do not range far from electric charging sources. So, they are not used in the same ways as a personal car.

If you have ever traveled on an electric-powered bicycle or scooter, you have used the same technology that is being developed in some electric cars. Electric cars emit no carbon dioxide. However, it is usually coal that is burned to produce the electricity they use, so using an electric car does increase one's carbon footprint. On the other hand, electrical cars may be carbon neutral if they are charged using a renewable source, such as solar energy. Charging electric cars from the current in someone's home is a possibility that researchers are developing. Although using house current creates a greater carbon footprint, it is still significantly smaller than one made by using gasoline.

Fuel Cells

A hydrogen fuel cell is a device that uses a chemical reaction between hydrogen and oxygen to produce electricity. The reaction produces only water and heat as waste by-products, so a car that runs on hydrogen fuel cells produces no carbon dioxide.

Why are fuel cells not used to power all of our cars? There are some drawbacks. First, fuel cells are very expensive. Presently, the cost of a car that runs on fuel cells is too much for most consumers. Second, unlike an electrical battery, a fuel cell requires a supply of fuel—oxygen and hydrogen—to create electricity. So, hydrogen must be stored in the vehicle, making the car too large and heavy to be practical. Finally, the hydrogen fuel needed to run the car has to be pumped, just as we currently pump gas. It will be a long time—if ever—before the United States develops the stations, pipelines, and delivery systems that are needed to deliver hydrogen.

Even though there are drawbacks to hydrogen fuel cells, governments and companies are devoting billions of dollars to developing and researching fuel cell technology. In 2006, for example, the U.S. government started the Hydrogen Fuel Initiative. The goal of this program is to make affordable and practical cars that run on fuel cell technology by the year 2020.

This is the engine compartment of an electric car that uses hydrogen fuel cell technology. The fuel tank, filled with hydrogen, is located in the trunk.

Ethanol Fuels

Imagine running your car with corn! Ethanol is an alcohol product that can be made from corn and used as fuel. When mixed with gasoline, ethanol provides an alternative to running a vehicle on fossil fuel alone. In the United States, there is some controversy regarding using corn to make ethanol fuels. Many experts argue that the production of a gallon of ethanol requires more energy and releases more carbon into the

Get Involved

Use the information you have learned about alternative fuels and take action in your community. Write to your local government officials, congressperson, or senator. The state of California adopted laws requiring vehicles to have lower carbon emissions. You can write letters to ask lawmakers to pass similar laws in your own state. Forcing the issue and making your voice heard may speed up the pace of research and development for better forms of energy. Check the resources in the "For More Information" section in the back of this book (pages 40–42) to track down the names and addresses of people you can write to about alternative fuels and global warming.

You can also write letters to car companies to let them know what kinds of vehicles you would like to see in the future. Let them know that the environment is important to you. In your letters, be sure to mention your age, as it sends a very powerful message when young people express their desire for a cleaner, better environment. Explain why you think it is important to develop new forms of fuel. If you support one kind over the others, say why. If you get your friends involved, the messages will come across louder and stronger than if you do it alone, and change is more likely to happen when people act together.

atmosphere than the production of a gallon of fossil fuel. Others argue that ethanol is causing food prices to rise as a result of extra corn production.

Despite the controversy, many consider ethanol a good alternative to fossil fuels. In Brazil, some vehicles run on ethanol only. In other countries, cars have engines that can switch back and forth from running on ethanol alone, gasoline alone, or a mixture of the two. This kind of car is useful because drivers can fill up with whatever fuel is available wherever they are.

Biomass and Biofuel

"Biomass" is a term that refers to matter that was once living, like firewood. Biofuel is fuel that comes from biomass material. Many sources of biomass can be regrown easily, so biofuels are a renewable source of energy. Although burning biofuels emits some carbon dioxide, these fuels are becoming more popular because they are an alternative to nonrenewable fossil fuels.

Another good thing about biofuels is they come from plants, which must absorb carbon dioxide from the atmosphere to live and grow. After absorbing carbon dioxide during their lifetimes, biofuel plants can be recycled and used as a renewable energy source. There are many forms of biofuel. Some engines designed to run in warm climates can run on pure vegetable oil, chicken fat, or other food waste products. One experimental biofuel vehicle traveled across the Sahara desert on discarded chocolate!

What the Future Holds

When people think about the first automobile, the first steam locomotive, or the first airplane flight, they think about progress. All of these were amazing inventions that improved lives and made society more advanced. They were a solution to our transportation problems. Today, we must think of new solutions to our transportation problems. We must think about how to rely less on carbon-based fuels that harm the environment.

In 2004, students from Middlebury College in Vermont drove this converted biodiesel school bus across the United States to raise awareness about alternate energy.

We must think about finding renewable, clean, and reliable energy sources.

You now know about practical ways to reduce your carbon footprint while going to school, soccer practice, or the store. And you know ways to reduce your carbon footprint as you travel on family vacations. It's important, now, to put this knowledge to work. Without action, all the knowledge in the world cannot lessen the effects of global warming or improve the state of our planet.

Glossary

biofuel Fuel that comes from biomass materials.

biomass Matter that was once living.

carbon-based When speaking of carbon footprints, a method that uses a fossil fuel.

carbon dioxide Colorless, odorless gas that is naturally present in the air.

carbon footprint Amount of carbon dioxide a person, group, corporation, or nation emits into the atmosphere, measured in pounds or tons.

carbon neutral Describing a person or object with no carbon footprint.

carbon offset Actions a person or group can take to make up for carbon emissions.

carpool Arrangement between people to travel together.

emissions Substances, such as gases, released into the air.

ethanol Alcohol product made from material such as corn.

fossil fuels Fuels formed under Earth's surface, including oil, coal, and natural gas.

fuel cell Device that uses a chemical reaction to produce electricity.

fuel-efficient Getting good gas mileage.

global warming Gradual warming of Earth's atmosphere.

hybrid When referring to vehicles, one that has two different sources of power.

hydrogen Colorless, odorless gas used to power fuel cells.

solar cells Devices that convert the sun's rays into electricity.

solar energy Energy from the sun's rays.

For More Information

Clean Air Watch
1250 Connecticut Avenue NW, Suite 200
Washington, DC 20036
(202) 558-3527
Web site: http://www.cleanairwatch.org
Clean Air Watch is a national nonprofit organization working to protect clean air
   laws and policies throughout the United States.

Environment Canada
Inquiry Centre
70 Cremazie Street
Gatineau, QC K1A 0H3
Canada
(800) 668-6767
E-mail: enviroinfo@ec.gc.ca
Web site: http://www.ec.gc.ca
Environment Canada is the department of the Canadian government responsible for
   issuing weather forecasts and warnings and monitoring Canada's environmental
   policies.

Environmental Protection Agency (EPA)
1200 Pennsylvania Avenue NW
Washington, DC 20460
(800) 424-4372

Web site: http://www.epa.gov/climatechange/emissions/ind_
    calculator.html
The EPA works to protect the environment of the United States. Its Web site has a
    personal emissions calculator for figuring out your carbon footprint.

Global Green USA
2218 Main Street, 2nd Floor
Santa Monica, CA 90405
(310) 581-2700
E-mail: ggusa@globalgreen.org
Web site: http://www.globalgreen.org
Global Green is an environmental organization addressing climate change.

National Geographic Society/National Geographic Kids
1145 17th Street NW
Washington, DC 20036
(800) 647-5463
Web site: http://kids.nationalgeographic.com
National Geographic Kids is a magazine and Web site sponsored by the National
    Geographic Society. It includes information about global warming and the
    environment.

Natural Resources Defense Council
40 West 20th Street
New York, NY 10011
(212) 727-2700

E-mail: nrdcinfo@nrdc.org

Web site: http://www.nrdc.org

This environmental action agency works to protect wildlife, wilderness areas, and
clean air and water.

Web Sites

Due to the changing nature of Internet links, Rosen Publishing has
developed an online list of Web sites related to the subject of this book.
This site is updated regularly. Please use this link to access the list:

http://www.rosenlinks.com/ycf/omgt

For Further Reading

Cherry, Lynnen, and Gary Braasch. *How We Know What We Know About Our Changing Climate: Scientists and Kids Explore Global Warming.* Nevada City, CA: Dawn Publications, 2008.

David, Laurie, and Cambria Gordon. *The Down-to-Earth Guide to Global Warming.* New York, NY: Orchard Books, 2007.

Jankeliowitch, Anne. *For Earth's Sake: 50 Ideas to Help Save the Planet.* New York, NY: Harry Abrams, Inc., 2008.

Murphy, Glenn. *A Kid's Guide to Global Warming.* New York, NY: Barnes and Noble, 2008.

Thornhill, Jan. *This Is My Planet: The Kids' Guide to Global Warming.* Ontario, Canada: Maple Tree Press, 2007.

Time magazine editors. *Global Warming: The Causes, the Perils, the Solutions, the Actions: 51 Things You Can Do.* New York, NY: Time, 2007.

Wines, Jacquie. *You Can Save the Planet: 50 Ways You Can Make a Difference.* New York, NY: Scholastic, 2008.

Bibliography

Amtrak. "What Is a Carbon Footprint?" Retrieved August 8, 2007 (http://www.amtrak.com/servlet/Satellite?c=WSArticlePage&cid=1173376444452&pagename=WhistleStop/WSArticlePage/Blank_Template).

California Environmental Protection Agency Air Resources Board. "LEV II—Amendments to California's Low Emission Vehicle Regulations." November 23, 2004. Retrieved January 10, 2008 (http://www.arb.ca.gov/msprog/levprog/levii/factsht.htm).

CarbonFootprint.com "What Is a Carbon Footprint?" Retrieved August 15, 2007 (http://www.carbonfootprint.com/carbonfootprint.html).

Caselli, Irene. "Chocolate Fuels a Carbon-Negative Voyage from England to Timbuktu." Yahoo! News, December 21, 2007. Retrieved January 10, 2008 (http://news.yahoo.com/s/csm/20071221/ts_csm/obiotruck).

CNN. "Diesels Aren't Dirty Anymore." December 12, 2007. Retrieved December 13, 2007 (http://www.cnn.com/2007/LIVING/wayoflife/12/12/aa.diesels.not.dirty/index.html).

CNN. "Rule Will Force NYC Taxis to Go Green." December 12, 2007. Retrieved December 12, 2007 (http://www.cnn.com/2007/TECH/science/12/12/green.taxis.ap/index.html).

Cruickshank, Douglas. "One Small Step: How to Measure a Carbon Footprint." Edutopia, October 3, 2007. Retrieved January 10, 2008 (http://www.edutopia.org/one-small-step-measure-carbon-footprint).

David, Laurie, and Cambria Gordon. *The Down-to-Earth Guide to Global Warming*. New York, NY: Orchard Books, 2007.

Environment News Service. "New York City Tallies Its Greenhouse Gas Emissions." April 11, 2007. Retrieved November 12, 2007 (http://www.ens-newswire.com/ens/apr2007/2007-04-11.asp).

Global Tech Forum. "Flight of Fancy?" March 10, 2006. Retrieved November 12, 2007 (http://globaltechforum.eiu.com/index.asp?layout=rich_story&channelid=3&categoryid=10&title=Flight+of+fancy%3F&doc_id=8289).

Henry Ford Museum. "The Life of Henry Ford." 2003. Retrieved November 7, 2007 (http://www.hfmgv.org/exhibits/hf).

How Stuff Works. "How Fuel Cells Work." Retrieved November 12, 2007 (http://auto.howstuffworks.com/fuel-cell.htm).

How Stuff Works. "How Much Fuel Does an International Plane Use for a Trip?" Retrieved November 28, 2007 (http://travel.howstuffworks.com/question192.htm).

McKibben, Bill. *Fight Global Warming Now: Your Handbook for Taking Action in Your Community*. New York, NY: Henry Holt and Company, 2007.

MSNBC. "Hybrid-Car Sales Growth Slowed in 2006." February 26, 2007. Retrieved November 28, 2007 (http://www.msnbc.msn.com/id/17346041).

MTA New York City Transit. "Subways." Retrieved January 24, 2008 (http://mta.info/nyct/facts/ffsubway.htm).

NYC Visit. "NYC Statistics." Retrieved November 21, 2007 (http://www.nycvisit.com/content/index.cfm?pagePkey=57).

Ratcliff, Evan. "The Plant That Will Save America." *Wired*, Vol. 15, No. 10, October 2007, pp. 158–167.

Shepard, Anna. "Shrink Your Carbon Footprint." Times Online. Retrieved January 24, 2008 (http://women.timesonline.co.uk/tol/life_and_style/women/body_and_soul/article1679066.ece).

Transport for London. "London Trams." Retrieved November 12, 2007 (http://www.tfl.gov.uk/modalpages/2674.aspx).

U.S. Department of Transportation. Bureau of Transportation Statistics. Retrieved November 12, 2007 (http://www.bts.gov/publications/national_transportation_statistics/html/table_01_11.html).

U.S. Environmental Protection Agency. "Extreme Events." December 20, 2007. Retrieved January 10, 2008 (http://epa.gov/climatechange/effects/extreme.html).

WashingtonPost.com. "10 Other Great Biking Cities." October 1, 2006. Retrieved October 29, 2007 (http://www.washingtonpost.com/wpdyn/contne/article/2006/09/29/AR2006092900490.html).

White, Joseph B. "Hybrid or All-Electric? Car Makers Take Sides." *Wall Street Journal*, October 24, 2007.

Wildman, Sarah. "Save Time and Savor the Countryside." *New York Times*, September 17, 2007.

World Fact Book. "United States: Population/Transportation." February 12, 2008. Retrieved February 22, 2008 (https://www.cia.gov/library/publications/the-world-factbook/print/us.html).

Index

About the Authors

Kathy Furgang and Adam Furgang wrote about environmental issues in *Leonardo DiCaprio: Environmental Champion*, also published by Rosen. The couple lives near Albany, New York, with their two young sons. For ten years, Kathy Furgang has been a writer and editor of science books and textbooks for both students and teachers. The many topics she has written about include conservation, recycling, biodiversity, and renewable energy.

Photo Credits

Cover (top left) © Syracuse Newspapers/The Image Works; cover (top right) © David Paul Morris/Getty Images; cover (bottom) © Stefano Paltera/American Solar Challenge/Getty Images; p. 5 © www.istockphoto.com/David Lewis; pp. 7, 11 © www.istockphoto.com/Luis Carlos Torres; p. 8 © David McNew/Getty Images; p. 9 © Jonathan Maus/BikePortland.org; p. 13 © Bob Pepping/Contra Costa Times/Newscom; pp. 15, 21 © Tim Boyle/Getty Images; p. 16 © David Cooper/Toronto Star/Zuma Press; p. 18 © Joe Sohm/The Image Works; pp. 23, 29 © www.istockphoto.com/gocosmonaut; p. 24 Shutterstock.com; p. 27 © Austin Brown/Stone/Getty Images; pp. 31, 32 © Mark Zimmerman/Getty Images; p. 35 © Car Culture/Getty Images; p. 38 © AP Images.

Designer: Les Kanturek; Editor: Christopher Roberts
Photo Researcher: Amy Feinberg